DEPARTMENT OF HEALTH

The Care of Children

Principles and Practice in Regulations and Guidance

A NEW FRAMEWORK FOR THE CARE
AND UPBRINGING OF CHILDREN

LONDON: HMSO

© Crown copyright 1990
First published 1990
Third impression 1991

ISBN 0 11 321289 5

foreword

The principle that the welfare of the child comes first is the foundation of the responsibilities of social services authorities towards children. Translating this broad legal principle into practice requires us to unpack the concept of welfare into its component parts: firstly, in a general way for all children and, subsequently, for the individual children to whom social services authorities owe duties of protection and care. Developing a detailed understanding of a child's needs, identity and best interests enable us to take the action required to meet and fulfil them.

This understanding is important to those in central government who shape regulations and guidance. It is important also to all those in local government, voluntary organisations and private agencies who plan and provide services for children. The Children Act 1989 both places a duty and offers an opportunity unparalleled in our generation to identify those principles which should underpin all our work with children and families.

The Social Services Inspectorate, as part of its development programme on planning for children, invited Jane Rowe and an advisory group of social work academics and experienced practitioners to produce a guide to the principles of good child care. This was intended to assist practitioners and supervisors to relate law to practice and to understand the context in which regulations and guidance were issued. The Children Bill reached its final stages while the guide was being prepared. Its remit was accordingly extended to incorporate the new Children Act 1989 with its forthcoming regulations and guidance.

The completed guide is a valuable foundation for practice in implementing the Children Act 1989. It should be read and used alongside the Introduction to the Children Act 1989 (HMSO), and regulations and guidance as they are issued.

W B Utting
Chief Inspector
Social Services Inspectorate
Department of Health

THE ADVISORY GROUP

Wendy Rose (*Chairman*)	Assistant Chief Inspector Social Services Inspectorate Department of Health
Jane Rowe OBE	Child Care Researcher Project Consultant
Dr Jane Aldgate	Lecturer and Fellow of St Hilda's College, Oxford
Dr Carolyn Davies	Principal Research Officer Department of Health
Philip Douglas	Operations Manager Northamptonshire County Council Social Services Department
John Fitzgerald OBE	Director The Bridge Child Care Consultancy Service
Jim Furniss	Principal Community Services Division CS3A Department of Health
Geoff Gildersleeve	Social Services Inspector Department of Health
John Goldup	Family Services Manager London Borough of Islington Social Services Department
Jeff Hopkins	Lecturer Department of Applied Social Studies and Social Work Keele University
Brother James	Catholic Child Welfare Society Diocese of Middlesbrough
Geoffrey James	Social Services Inspector Department of Health
Jim Kennedy	Social Services Inspector Department of Health
Barbara K Lerner	Development Officer Hertfordshire County Council Social Services Department
Ruth Prime	Social Services Inspector Department of Health
John Reed	Executive Officer Community Services Division CS3A
Paul Sutton	Director Birmingham Action on Child Care City of Birmingham Social Services Department
June Thoburn	Senior Lecturer University of East Anglia

contents

FOREWORD BY   W B Utting   iii
                        Chief Inspector
                        Social Services Inspectorate

THE MEMBERS OF THE ADVISORY GROUP   iv

1. INTRODUCTION   1

The Status of Regulations and Guidance   2
Their Focus, Range and Depth   3

2. THE PRINCIPLES OF GOOD CHILD CARE PRACTICE   7

Principles in Relation to Individual Children and Young People and their Families   7
Principles in Relation to Agency Responsibilities and Systems   12

3. THE PRINCIPLES AND REGULATIONS IN PRACTICE   16

APPENDIX   18

Summarised List of Principles   18

CHAPTER 1   INTRODUCTION

The passing of the Children Act 1989 is likely to prove a watershed in the history of British child care. It both reflects and requires major changes in attitudes and practice. However, the Act itself provides only part of the legal and administrative framework within which social services for children and families will be provided in the 1990s. Before the implementation date of October 1991, there will be many new sets of regulations and guidance which will supersede all existing regulations and cover a wide range of child care issues.

Questions about the status of such documents have already been triggered off by the Boarding Out and Charge and Control Regulations (1988) and the guidance which accompanied them. Are these legal requirements which must be complied with by social services departments and individual social workers? Or are they merely guidelines setting out targets to be reached, if possible? And what about 'Working Together' the guide on inter-agency work in child abuse cases, also published in 1988, or the statutory code of practice 'Access to Children in Care' which came out in 1983 but is still not familiar to all practitioners? Are these more or less binding than regulations?

There are queries, too, about how comprehensive the law, regulations, codes and guidance are intended to be. Is the faithful carrying out of what they require sufficient to ensure good practice? How much is left to local policy and procedures or to professional discretion? Why are some matters dealt with in so much detail even though they seem relatively unimportant while other, major issues rate only a few lines?

Such questions become even more pressing in the light of the new Children Act and all the documents which will flow from it, so this guide is an attempt to provide some answers and to show how law, regulations, codes and guidance relate to the principles of good child care practice which have been developed over time and distilled from research and practice wisdom. The very fundamental changes in thinking and in policy, practice and terminology which the implementation of the Act will demand, make this seem a particularly important time to publish a set of basic principles. Without the firm ground of agreed and well understood principles, there is a risk that those involved in the child care service will feel overwhelmed and bewildered by the extent and speed of change required.

Like the new Act itself, the principles set out in this guide seek to encompass an understanding of Britain's multi-ethnic and multi-cultural society in the 1990s. It is essential that practitioners should seek to combat racism as well as other forms of discrimination against individuals and groups. The Act encourages this approach. Partnership, participation, choice, openness, parental responsibility and every child's need for both security and family links are some of the major themes which are common to the principles and to the legislation.

Because it is being written after the passing of the Act but while the old laws and regulations are still in force, this guide has to straddle the fence with regard to examples and terminology. In Part I, most references are to existing regulations and guidance documents even though they are likely to be extensively revised and will be reissued under new titles.

The principles set out and discussed in Chapters II & III will not in themselves be affected by the legal changes except that the new Act seeks to reflect them more fully than the former statutes did and this process should be further enhanced by new regulations and guidance. Therefore, in these later sections of the paper, it seems helpful to make further references to the new Act and to move forward to the use of new terminology and new concepts. So, for example, the concept of 'access' is replaced by 'contact', 'in care' is used only for children and young people in compulsory care and the phrases 'being looked after by the local authority' or 'in accommodation' are used to include what has been known as voluntary care even though there are some major differences.

THE STATUS OF REGULATIONS AND GUIDANCE

The status of principal legislation such as the Children Act 1989 is generally clearly understood. It is the law and must be obeyed. But the status of regulations, codes and guidance is less well appreciated

Regulations are what is called subordinate legislation. They are made by the Lord Chancellor or Secretary of State under the authority of an Act which is primary legislation. Thus the Boarding-Out and Charge and Control Regulations 1988 were both made under the authority of the Child Care Act 1980 and the 1986 Amendment Act, and the Children Act 1989 gives the Secretary of State power to issue a wide range of regulations.

Regulations have 'the full force of a statute' (*Halsbury's 'Laws of England'*). This means that they must be obeyed as law under all circumstances. They include permissions and restrictions as to what may or may not be done and also requirements on what must be done.

Guidance documents and circulars are usually issued as general guidance of the Secretary of State as described in S7(1) of the Local Authority Social Services Act 1970. Local authorities are required to act in accordance with such guidance which is intended to be a statement of what is held to be good practice. Though they are not in themselves law in the way that regulations are law, guidance documents are likely to be quoted or used in court proceedings as well as in local authority policy and practice papers. They could provide the basis for a legal challenge of an authority's action or inaction, including (in extreme cases) default action by the Secretary of State.

Guidance is often issued alongside regulations, e.g. the handbooks that accompany the Boarding-Out and Charge and Control Regulations. But guidance documents may also stand alone, e.g. 'Working Together'.

Codes of practice fall between regulations and guidance notes. They may be 'statutory' in that they are required by legislation and are laid before Parliament. They therefore carry more weight than other departmental guidance, but they are not law in the way that regulations are law. As with Section 7 guidance, courts expect detailed justification for not following codes of practice, but some flexibility to suit the needs of a particular case is allowed and expected.

One might sum up the differences between the requirements of these various official documents like this:— Regulations say '*You must/shall*'; codes say '*You ought/should*'. When guidance explains regulations, it reaffirms the '*you must*' messages. However, when it goes beyond regulations in setting out good practice, it conveys the message that '*It is highly desirable to...*' or '*Unless there is good reason not to, you should...*' rather than '*You must*'.

THEIR FOCUS RANGE AND DEPTH

Even when regulations and guidance documents are issued under the same Act, they may have rather different approaches to their topics and vary in depth and detail. They may also grow from very different roots. Thus the Boarding-Out Regulations 1988 drew together the cumulative experience of decades of fostering, going back to the nineteenth century. They could build on previous regulations, whereas the Charge and Control Regulations which were published at the same time, had to start from scratch and there was very little written theory or 'practice wisdom' to draw on. Then, too, the Boarding-Out Regulations arose from gradual changes and developments in practice, whereas Charge and Control Regulations and the guidance paper 'Working Together' sprang from recent, specific problems, while the code of practice on access sought to deal with old problems in the light of changing attitudes. Another quite striking difference is that the code on access offers general guidance on how to think and how to approach potential problems over family links for children in care whereas 'Working Together' gives specific instruction on what to do to set up inter-disciplinary and inter-departmental arrangements for dealing with child abuse.

In relation to child care placements, there seem to be four potential areas of concern:
(1) The provision of a service;
(2) 'Managing' placements;
(3) Meeting the child's general needs;
(4) Creating a particular placement experience.

The first two areas can be fairly easily dealt with by regulation and so, to a lesser extent, can meeting general needs. By contrast, creating a particular placement experience for an individual child must always be a matter of skill and judgement and cannot be regulated.

The focus of the current Boarding-Out Regulations and guidance is as much on providing a foster care service as it is on managing placements. On the other hand, the Charge and Control Regulations and guidance are almost entirely concerned with the 'management' of placements and have little or nothing to say about providing a service. Similar differences appear between the code on access and 'Working Together'. The code deals in general terms with parent/child links in any kind of in-care placement. It falls mainly into the category of meeting children's general needs but has some relevant things to say about managing placements and provision of basic services. While it cannot deal with the practice of creating a particular placement experience, it clearly recognises the individuality of children's needs and wishes. 'Working Together' has quite a different approach. It is mainly about systems and is limited to just one aspect of work with abused children and their families. In setting out systems for co-operative case management, 'Working Together' provides a structure for decision making, but it does not attempt to address the issues on which decisions must be made.

These comments are a statement of fact, not a criticism. It is obvious that neither regulations nor guidance can cover all the professional issues even though all guidance is intended to be read in the context of other guidance. Not only is their focus deliberately limited, but certain explicit and implicit assumptions have to be made. Many basic principles of child care fall into the implicit assumptions category. For example, s.1 (3) (c) of the Children Act 1989 is the first time that the importance for the child of maintaining continuity of relationships has received explicit attention in legislation or guidance except in the code on access. For the most part, the need for continuity has been implicit in the welfare principle to which reference is frequently made. This background of implicit assumptions needs to be borne in mind when regulations and guidance are put into practice or used as the basis for policies or procedures.

There are other inevitable restrictions on what regulations can include. A major one is that they have to be universal, enforceable, and are expected to be achievable within current constraints. This means that they can never really be 'best practice' but only 'good enough' practice. Guidance can aim higher, but guidance, too, may be limited by its primary purpose which is usually to explain the application of regulations.

It is also necessary to recognise that regulations and guidance have to deal with children in general and must leave it to professional practice to consider the particular needs which arise from differences of age, sex, ethnic and cultural background, life experience and personality. Thus even such a crucial issue as the specific needs of black and minority ethnic children can only be referred to briefly in regulations which cannot appropriately deal with these matters in the detail necessary to ensure good practice.

Regulations and procedures have to be drafted in terms of the best interests of the child. However, children do not develop in isolation but through interaction with others. *So whatever the specific purpose of a child care regulation or practice, it is always necessary to set consideration of an individual child's needs into a social context in which relationships are of central significance.*

Aspects of a service or task which are not covered by regulations may not get much attention from guidance documents since they do not purport to be detailed manuals of professional practice. Thus the Boarding-Out Regulations 1988 list topics to be included in enquiries about prospective foster parents, but they do not discuss what responses would be acceptable nor how this information can best be elicited. These matters are left open so that social services departments can develop their own policies over such things as age limits, marital status, a record of past, minor offences, etc. Much is also left open for the exercise of social work judgement, the assumption being that such judgement will be based on professional knowledge and skill.

Thus inevitably and intentionally, there is some room for manoeuvre within the confines of legislation, regulations and guidance. The question that has to be asked is: 'Once the legal requirements have been set, how much variation of policy and practice is acceptable?' It seems clear that if the needs of individual children and families are going to be met in an appropriate and sensitive way, flexibility is essential and rigid policies and procedures should be avoided. But unless flexibility is firmly based not only on an understanding of the legal framework, but also on shared principles, there will be no proper support for good practice. Indeed, flexibility can degenerate into inconsistency which is rightly perceived as both unjust and incompetent. An agreed set of principles can therefore be seen as one of the essential foundations of a good child care service.

Child care principles have been developed over a long period and have many roots. These roots include legal concepts; belief in the intrinsic value of each individual; knowledge from child development, psychology and psychiatry; practice wisdom; social research; prevailing community values.

At present, the welfare principle (*Child Care Act 1980 s.18*) provides the statutory basis for both legal decisions and professional practice. It states:

> '*In reaching any decision relating to a child in their care, a local authority shall give first consideration to the need to safeguard and promote the welfare of the child throughout his childhood; and shall so far as practicable ascertain the wishes and feelings of the child regarding the decision and give due consideration to them, having regard to his age and understanding.*'

As an overall statement this could hardly be bettered, but when it comes to making specific plans or decisions it is insufficiently detailed and explicit.

In the new Children Act, further details are given on the duties of courts and local authorities. Section 1 states that when a court is determining any question with respect to a child's upbringing, that child's welfare is to be the paramount consideration. It goes on to list the particular matters to which the court should pay regard. These include:

(a) the ascertainable wishes and feelings of the child concerned (considered in the light of his age and understanding);
(b) his physical, emotional and educational needs;
(c) the likely effect on him of any change in his circumstances;
(d) his age, sex, background and any characteristics of his which the court considers relevant;
(e) any harm which he has suffered or is at risk of suffering;
(f) how capable each of his parents, and any other person in relation to whom the court considers the question to be relevant, is of meeting his needs;

The duties laid on local authorities in relation to children in their care or accommodated by them are prescribed in more general terms. *Section 22(3)* states:

> 'It shall be the duty of a local authority looking after any child:
> (a) to safeguard and promote his welfare; and
> (b) to make such use of services available for children cared for by their own parents as appears to the authority reasonable in his case.'

Before making any decision with respect to a child whom they are looking after, local authorities are required (*so far as is reasonably practicable*), to ascertain the wishes and feelings of the child, his parents (*or others carrying parental responsbility*), and other persons whose wishes and feelings are considered relevant, with regard to the matter to be decided. Having ascertained these wishes and feelings, authorities are required to take them into consideration. Other matters which must be considered are the child's religious persuasion, racial origin and cultural and linguistic background.

It is a big step forward to have these very important matters incorporated into primary legislation where they can provide a firm legal basis for policy and planning. However, when it comes to working with individual children and families, the requirements are still too generalised so more detailed and specific principles are also needed.

Principles need to be distinguished from aims, policies and practice directions even though they form the basis for them. Thus 'prevention' and 'permanence' are aims, methods or policies which are derived from a combination of principles but 'paramountcy' of the child's welfare is a single, identifiable principle of child care law.

It may be helpful to think of principles as the colours on the social work painter's palette to be used in the combinations and patterns required for each picture painted/child care case handled. Social workers need to be as familiar with the principles of good child care as painters are with the colours in their paint box.

When the principles are integral to a social worker's thinking, they can be applied even in working conditions that are likely to be much more stressful than a painter's studio.

However, it would be wrong to imply that it is always easy to translate principles into practice. By their very nature, principles cannot be flexible, but they will not carry equal weight under all circumstances and actual conflict of principles can and does occur. Priorities must then be set according to individual circumstances and needs. Principles must never be applied blindly but used intelligently with common sense and sensitivity because it can be dangerous to over-emphasize any one principle to the extent that others are ignored or flouted. (*Some of the more usual dilemmas are discussed in Chapter III of this guide.*)

It is the responsibility of managers to be fully conversant with these principles and to base their policies and agency guidelines on them. Managers also have to provide the means by which the principles can be put into practice and ensure that this happens. The necessary resources include knowledge and skill and opportunities for consultation with senior social work staff, outside consultants, knowledgeable people from minority communities and experts from other disciplines as appropriate. Time is, of course, an essential resource and user-friendly buildings and adequate equipment are other important elements in enabling principles to be carried into daily work with children and their families.

CHAPTER 2 THE PRINCIPLES OF GOOD CHILD CARE PRACTICE

These principles apply to all social work with children and their families and are not confined to services such as fostering which are covered by regulations. They are presently governed by the welfare principle contained in s.18 of the Child Care Act 1980 quoted above, and amplify it by detailing areas in which safeguards and protections are needed and areas in which promotional actions are necessary, e.g. for children with special needs. All should be read and applied in the light of the overarching welfare principle.

The Appendix provides a list of all the 42 principles in an abbreviated form suitable for teaching or for group discussion.

PRINCIPLES IN RELATION TO INDIVIDUAL CHILDREN AND YOUNG PEOPLE AND THEIR FAMILIES*

(*To avoid tedious repetition, the terms 'children' and 'young people' are used interchangeably and either or both should be assumed to cover the whole age range 0–18 years.)

1) *Children and young people and their parents should all be considered as individuals with particular needs and potentialities.* Whilst clear policies and guidelines are necessary and helpful, standardised, routine decisions or rigid across-the-board policies do not lead to acceptable practice. All regulations, policies, guidance and procedures should take into account the wide diversity of ages, needs, ethnic origins, cultures and circumstances that lies behind general categories such as 'foster children', 'children in care', or 'children in need'.

2) *Although some basic needs are universal, there can be a variety of ways of meeting them.* Patterns of family life differ according to culture, class and community and these differences should be respected and accepted. There is no one, perfect way to bring up children and care must be taken to avoid value judgements and stereotyping.

3) *Children are entitled to protection from neglect. abuse and exploitation.* In Schedule 2 paragraph 4 of the Children Act 1989, local authorities are specifically required to "take reasonable steps...to prevent children within their area suffering ill-treatment or neglect." But all child care agencies have a duty to provide protection as necessary whether the danger comes from unrelated adults, from members of the child's family, from other caregivers or from 'systems' and bureaucracies. Young people's safety cannot be assumed just because their caregivers are known to the agency, and social workers who are responsible for children must remain alert to potential risks.

4) *A child's age, sex, health, personality, race, culture and life experiences are all relevant to any consideration of needs and vulnerability and have to be taken into account when planning or providing help.* (The Children Act 1989 recognises this in the emphasis on prevention of harm rather than proving specific acts against the child.) Some children are very resilient and find their own ways of coping which should be respected. Others are temperamentally sensitive and easily upset while traumatic experiences may make others prone to greater than average

fears of loss or rejection. Either personality, life experiences or inappropriate placement, or a combination of these, may result in provocative behaviour which also makes a child or young person vulnerable to scapegoating or retaliation by peers or adults.

Some children may require special care and protection because of their tender age or because they are ill, disabled or handicapped. Others may be extra vulnerable because of particular circumstances, e.g. those placed outside their own ethnic/cultural background; those who are separated from siblings or disconnected from their family networks.

5) *There are unique advantages for children in experiencing normal family life in their own birth family and every effort should be made to preserve the child's home and family links.* A wide variety of services, including short-term out-of-home placement, may need to be employed in order to sustain some families through particularly difficult periods. The provision of services to help maintain the family home is a requirement of the Children Act 1989 (Schedule 2, para. 8, 9, 10.)

6) *Parents are individuals with needs of their own.* Even though services may be offered primarily on behalf of their children, parents are entitled to help and consideration in their own right. Just as some young people are more vulnerable than others, so are some mothers and fathers. Their parenting capacity may be limited temporarily or permanently by poverty, racism, poor housing or unemployment or by personal or marital problems, sensory or physical disability, mental illness or past life experiences. Lack of parenting skills or inability to provide adequate care should not be equated with lack of affection or with irresponsibility.

7) *The development of a working partnership with parents is usually the most effective route to providing supplementary or substitute care for their children.* Measures which antagonise, alienate, undermine or marginalise parents are counter-productive. For example, taking compulsory powers over children can all too easily have this effect though such action may be necessary in order to provide protection.

8) *Admission to public care by virtue of a compulsory order is in itself a risk to be balanced against others. So also is the accommodation of a child by a local authority.* If out-of-home placement is necessary, the least coercive legal status consistent with meeting the child's needs (including 'no order at all') should be the first choice; – likewise the least restrictive placement.

9) *If young people cannot remain at home, placement with relatives or friends should be explored before other forms of placement are considered.* Research has shown that placements with relatives are usually more successful than those made outside the family circle. However, family relationships can be negative and placements with relatives should not be made without adequate exploration and discussion nor as a way of saving money or keeping 'in care' figures low.

10) *If young people have to live apart from their family of origin, both they and their parents should be given adequate information and helped to consider alternatives and contribute to the making of an informed choice about the most appropriate form of care.* For most children and many young people, this is likely to be a family placement whether temporary or longer term, but some young people have a clear preference for group care

and some parents may at first feel threatened by the idea of a foster family caring for their child.

11) *When out-of-home care is necessary, active steps should be taken to ensure speedy return home.* The first six weeks after admission are crucial, and during this time social work effort needs to be maintained or even increased even though the immediate crisis may seem to be over.

12) *Parents should be expected and enabled to retain their responsibilties and to remain as closely involved as is consistent with their child's welfare, even if that child cannot live at home either temporarily or permanently.* (Sections 2, 3 & 4 of the Children Act 1989 explain parental responsibility. Section 33(3) expounds the concept of shared parental responsibility.) Parents should participate in decisions about their child and it should be exceptional for them not to be invited to reviews and case conferences. If they are not invited, the reasons for this should be explicit, justified and recorded. However, it must be recognised that attendance at such meetings can be daunting for parents, particularly if they will be the only black people present, if English is not their first language, or if they suffer from any form of disability. The presence of a friend, interpreter or advocate can provide useful support and facilitate communication.

13) *Siblings should not be separated when in care or when being looked after under voluntary arrangements, unless this is part of a well thought out plan based on each child's needs.* When large families require care away from home, every effort should be made to provide accommodation where they can remain together. However, a child's needs should not be sacrificed in order to meet those of a sibling.

14) *Family links should be actively maintained through visits and other forms of contact. Both parents are important even if one of them is no longer in the family home and fathers should not be overlooked or marginalised.* A parent's inability to sustain contact should not be assumed to be an indication of lack of interest and concern. Parents should be expected to keep in touch but are entitled to financial help and emotional support over visiting and other forms of contact. For some, visiting is painful and difficult. Research suggests that clear expectations of the timing and frequency of visits can provide useful support. Occasionally, contact between a child and one or more relatives may be destructive or even dangerous. In these rather rare circumstances, children must be protected and their needs considered paramount. In special circumstances an independent visitor may be appointed.

15) *Wider families matter as well as parents – especially siblings and grandparents.* Family friends may play an important part. Black families in particular may have 'aunties' and 'uncles' who have a close relationship with the child without being blood relatives. Links with individuals and the wider community can and should be maintained.

16) *Continuity of relationships is important, and attachments should be respected, sustained and developed.* While this is of primary concern in relation to family ties even when children may not be going home, it also applies to relationships with caregivers and social workers. Admission to care or changes of placement should not cause young people to lose touch with people who love them and who may be of help to them later on as well as

during the care experience. In the same way, meaningful relationships formed during a period in out-of-home care should, if at all possible, be maintained after discharge.

17) *Change of home, caregiver, social worker or school almost always carries some risk to a child's development and welfare.* Changes should be kept to a minimum and are not justified for bureaucratic convenience. When essential, changes should be made with care and sensitivity. The potentially beneficial aspect of a change, (e.g. for protection, for special treatment/education or for new opportunities), must be weighed against the potential damage of disrupted relationships and loss of security. Children and young people should be given as much security about their future as can possibly be achieved.

18) *Time is a crucial element in child care and should be reckoned in days and months rather than years.* Immature children cannot wait but need what they need when they need it. Providing it 'later' is often too late and the younger the child, the greater the urgency. For some adolescents, learning to wait for 'later' is part of growing up, but the wait should be based on the young person's need and not on the social worker's convenience or the bureaucracy's time scale. The Children Act 1989 specifically requires courts to avoid delay in child care cases.

19) *Every young person needs to develop a secure sense of personal identity and all those with parental or caring responsibilities have a duty to offer encouragement and support in this task.* Help may be provided by giving information essential to the young person's self knowledge or through experiences which enhance individual autonomy and confidence.

All children – whether living at home or not – are entitled to expect information about their personal and family history and need to understand their past as well as their present situation. They also need opportunities to develop independence and see themselves as competent individuals.

Young people whose families are fragmented or very disorganised, and those who are brought up outside their family of origin, face special difficulties in achieving a comfortable and secure identity. Problems may be particularly acute if there are major differences between children's birth families and their current life situation. The integration of what may be puzzling or painful information is likely to be a slow process. Life-story books can help, but will only provide a base for continuing work and can never really take the place of contact with parents, relatives and other important people from the child's past.

Young people from ethnic minorities will find it difficult to develop confidence and pride in their identity if this is constantly undermined or undervalued by individual or institutional racism. This can happen even when the racism is not deliberate and perhaps not even recognised by the perpetrator.

20) *All children need to develop self confidence and a sense of self worth, so alongside the development of identity, and equally important, is self esteem.* The questions 'Who am I?' and 'How do I feel about myself?' continue throughout life, but are particularly prominent during adolescence. Identity develops from knowledge and from understanding of one's place in the scheme of things, while self esteem is largely based on the perceived reactions of other people. Those who feel unloved, unwanted,

belittled or discriminated against will have their self esteem undermined.

Young people who have to live outside their family of origin are likely to have their self esteem damaged by the circumstances which led to their placement especially as they may quite inappropriately blame themselves for what has happened. Some feel 'labelled' by being in public care.

Those who suffer from any form of disability may also have low self esteem. They are entitled to opportunities to develop their abilities, to use their often hard-won achievements and skills and to be accepted as valued members of the community.

Special issues arise for young black people and those from minority ethnic groups. They need to develop a self image which is positive and includes their ethnic and cultural origins which must be taken into consideration by both planners and caregivers. If black children and those from ethnic minorities are placed in settings where issues of race are not acknowledged, they will be deprived of opportunities to discuss painful and confusing experiences of overt or covert racism and can become very insecure about their identity and self worth. Those of mixed parentage face particular problems. They are generally perceived by others as black yet need to integrate both strands of their heritage. Those who are brought up by their white parent or in a white family placement can find themselves experiencing an extra dimension to the normal problems and conflicts of adolescence. And if they have not had strong links with their community of origin, they may end up rejected by both groups.

21) *Since discrimination of all kinds is an everyday reality in many children's lives, every effort must be made to ensure that agency services and practices do not reflect or reinforce it.* Attention should be given to ways of equipping young people to cope with and resist the discrimination they experience. Ethnic minority children should be helped to be proud of their racial and cultural heritage. Those of minority religions need opportunities to understand, value and practice their faith. There are also important issues of gender and sexuality to be considered. Attention may need to be given to ensuring that girls have equal opportunities to develop as wide a variety of skills, interests and careers as boys, while both boys and girls need to be given a positive view of the adult roles which they can fulfill.

22) *Corporate parenting is not 'good enough' on its own.* Every child and young person needs at least one individual to whom s/he is 'special', who retains responsibility over time, who is involved in plans and decisions and who has ambitions for the child's achievement and full development. A parent or relative is most likely to fulfil this role, but if birth family members are not available, the care agency needs to identify suitable individuals and encourage them in the role. Efforts should be made to ensure that this individual will be available to any young person who is moving out of care at 18 and into adult life.

23) *Young people should not be disadvantaged or stigmatised by action taken on their behalf,* e.g. as a result of admission to care or accommodation, or to special residential provision. A sub-section of the welfare principle (Child Care Act 1980 s.18) specifically states that 'normal' provision (e.g. health, education and leisure services), should be used wherever possible and the

new Act builds this principle into the duties of local authorities toward children whom they are looking after (s.22(3)).

24) *Children's long-term welfare must be protected by prompt, positive and pro-active attention to the health and education of those in both short and long-term care.* Good physical care, including attention to minor ailments, and education in the widest sense of all-round personal development as well as schooling, are both important and should be taken seriously. The disadvantages that most children in public care have suffered and continue to suffer, require recognition and reparation through treatment, remedial work and teaching, and opportunities to develop skills and interests.

25) *Young people's wishes must be elicited and taken seriously.* Even quite young children should be enabled to contribute to decisions about their lives in an age appropriate way. Learning to make a well-informed choice is an important aspect of growing up and must involve more than just sitting in on reviews and conferences at which adults have all the power and make all the decisions. Young people in care should be given the chance to exercise choice and if they are unhappy about decisions or placements, they should have an opportunity to be heard and taken seriously.

26) *As young people grow up, preparation for independence is a necessary and important part of the parental role which child care agencies carry for young people in long-term care.* However, it is unrealistic to expect that most youngsters still in their teens can or should be entirely self-supporting and self-sufficient. This is a stage in life when young people need a home base to which they can return at intervals of their own choosing and on which they can rely for unobtrusive support when facing difficulties. A local authority or voluntary society which has been fulfilling all or most aspects of the parental role, has a responsibility to continue providing back-up support either directly or – often appropriately – via former carers. There should be no automatic cut-off of services or financial help when a young person formally leaves care at 18.

PRINCIPLES IN RELATION TO AGENCY RESPONSIBILITIES AND 'SYSTEMS'

27) *In carrying out the duties and responsibilities laid upon them in legislation and regulations, local authorities should put into practice the principles of good work with children and families* which are set out in the previous section. All the systems and procedures devised to accomplish the work should reflect the principles and, while providing a secure framework, must be sufficiently flexible to accommodate individual needs and circumstances.

28) *The various departments of a local authority (e.g. health, housing, education and social services) should co-operate to provide an integrated service and range of resources* even when such co-operation is not specifically required by law. This also applies to voluntary organisations.

29) *The twin issues of confidentiality and access to records need to be addressed by all local authorities and child care organisations.* Staff at all levels, foster carers and volunteers must be made fully aware of the need to respect the rights of adults and children to confidentiality over their personal affairs. On the other hand, children and adults (parents, staff, foster

carers) all need to know what information is held about them and what may be done with it. Agencies will need to develop their own policy, systems and procedures to deal with both access to information and the preservation of confidentiality.

30) *Caregivers are entitled to have appropriate information about any child or young person placed in their charge and have a duty to keep this confidential.* It is not only foster carers and residential staff who need information. Parents who are resuming care of their children who have been away from home for a while need to know about their experiences while away and the parenting and lifestyles to which they have become accustomed.

31) *Letters and documents which are sent to parents and young people should be written in language which is fully comprehensible to them.* This means using simple, non-bureaucratic English and, where necessary, translation into the recipient's mother tongue. If the recipient has a sensory disability, special arrangements will be needed for appropriate communication. The use of tapes, large print or braille may have to be considered.

32) *Planning is a central responsibility for all agencies providing services to children and their families.* This applies to children in their own homes as well as to those being looked after by a local authority or voluntary society. The following elements are important:-

   a) Planning must take the other principles into account.
   b) Assessment must precede planning.
   c) Plans should be regularly reassessed both informally and at reviews and case conferences in which young people, their parents and/or caregivers should normally be present. An absence of crisis or obvious problems is not necessarily synonymous with progress.
   d) Clarity and effective communication are essential and written agreements are likely to be the most effective method of achieving this. Decisions and the reasons for them should be recorded and notifications sent to the appropriate people.
   e) The goal must be inherent in the plan and clearly stated. Very prolonged assessment or a generalised 'wait and see' approach cannot be considered a 'plan'.

33) *Agencies have special, parental responsibilities for the minority of children who are in long-term out-of-home placements.* These include:– the need to provide a sense of permanence and security; experience of normal family life; provision for appropriate and sufficient education and training for a satisfying job; the development of personal skills, talents and interests; obtaining and passing on to the young person (preferably through direct contact with family members or previous carers) sufficient detailed background information to make possible a confident sense of identity and an understanding of the reasons for separation. Special attention is required in order to meet the needs of children from ethnic, cultural or religious minorities or those with disabilities. This includes ensuring that they attend schools where they will not be stereotyped, or assumed to have low levels of intelligence. It is the responsibility of agencies, and those to whom they entrust the care of children, to look into the attitudes of head teachers and staff toward issues of race, religion and culture or toward children with disabilities attending ordinary schools.

34) *When alternatives are being considered and/or decisions made, certain individuals or groups may need to be involved.* Sometimes this is laid

down in regulations, e.g. adoption panels or the requirement that a senior manager make decisions about 'charge and control' placements. At other times individual circumstances will determine who should be involved. Among those whose useful contribution may be overlooked are members of the wider family who are important to the child, past caregivers with special knowledge of the child's history, teachers or playgroup leaders, people with special knowledge of the ethnic issues, culture, religion or lifestyle appropriate for meeting the needs of the particular family or young person. It is important to keep decision making as close as possible to the child and carers and to find a balance between the need for full information and consideration and the risk of delay, diffusion of effort and difficulty in communication if decision making groups become too large.

35) Services to vulnerable children have to be largely provided through those who give them day to day care whether these are parents, relatives, residential social workers or foster carers. *In each case, a balance must be struck between offering carers support (thus building confidence) and holding them accountable for the child's well-being.* In developing an effective partnership with carers, clear communication, shared planning and written agreements are all necessary.

36) *Caregivers – whether parents, foster carers or residential staff – need both practical resources and a feeling of being valued if they are to give of their best.* Thought should be given to the need for respite care or babysitting and the developoment of support networks and foster carers' wish to help should not be exploited by pressure to take in additional children. When arrangements are being made for sustained or renewed contact with important people from the child's past, the comfort of all concerned – but especially the child and the long-term carers – must be taken into account.

37) *Appropriate training should be provided for carers.* This may range from teaching parenting and home-making skills by provision of a family aide, through to training courses for caregivers on a variety of topics including ethnic issues, communication skills, child development, disability or the special needs of abused or emotionally disturbed young people. The education/training of foster carers for their special tasks should be seen as an ongoing process in which the preparation courses for new foster carers and residential staff are only the beginning.

38) *There should be machinery for resolving differences of view* or minor disputes, e.g. through involvement of a team leader, fostering officer or other appropriate individual or through renegotiating written agreements at the request of any of the signatories. In addition, parents, relatives and foster parents should have a right of access to a more formal procedure the existence of which should be well publicised. (When the Children Act 1989 is implemented, procedures will be a statutory requirement.)

39) *Agencies have a responsibility to support placements which they have made.* While this is obvious in relation to placements of young people for whom the agency carries a legal responsibility, it may also apply to placements where supervision and support are not required by law, e.g. young people being brought up by relatives; those living independently or those at home after discharge of a care order. The deciding factor should be the child or young person's vulnerability and/or the caregivers' need for help. Shared care arrangements may need continuing support as well as help in negotiating and organising mutually acceptable plans for visits and contact.

40) *Registers and records must be maintained and kept up to date.* This is not just a question of efficiency – though this is important. Records are an essential tool for good practice and may also hold information of vital

importance to a young person's emotional well-being. Older people who were in care as children may also require detailed personal and family history for practical reasons and also for their mental health.

41) *Co-operation between organisations, departments and individuals is crucial* in the provision of protection for vulnerable children and also in ensuring proper use of available resources. Managers have a responsibility to ensure that the systems provided for such co-operation are not only known but also used appropriately because, at all levels of organisations, processes can be as important as objectives.

42) *Foster homes and residential establishments used for the placement of children should be reviewed at regular and suitable intervals* though this needs to be done sensitively so as to avoid undermining carers' confidence or making children feel insecure. Guidelines for such reviews should be clear about which aspects of the home or establishment are to be reviewed and should direct attention to areas which may be of particular concern in specific instances, e.g. when children with disabilities are being looked after; when secure accommodation is provided; if black youngsters have all or mainly white caregivers; if a number of unrelated children are being cared for in a foster home or if long stay and short stay children are accommodated together.

CHAPTER 3 THE PRINCIPLES AND REGULATIONS IN PRACTICE

The purpose of regulations is to require (or prohibit) certain actions or attitudes. Sometimes a regulation is a way of bringing a particular principle to bear on a situation. Examples of this are Boarding Out Regulation 5(3) and Charge and Control Regulation 8(3)(c). These regulations require the agency to pay attention to the child's cultural background and racial origin and thus directly reflect Principles 4, 19 & 20.

More often, the proper carrying out of a regulation involves reference to several principles and, if necessary, deciding on a hierarchy of importance. Thus the first duty of local authorities or voluntary societies in relation to foster placements is to satisfy themselves that a foster placement is the most suitable way of performing their duty toward a particular child. A number of principles have a bearing on this decision, e.g.:

1. A fostering plan should not be imposed routinely without consideration of alternatives.

4. The particular needs of this child must be studied.

10 & 25. Children and young people should be helped to make informed choices and their views on a fostering plan should be sought and taken seriously.

13–16. The effect of foster placement on family links and existing relationships must be considered.

10, 12 & 34. Parents' views about foster placement should be elicited and carefully considered.

According to individual circumstances, one of these principles may over-ride others. The weighing up of principles in specific situations calls for discernment and experience. A child's particular need for a certain form of treatment or education *might* over-ride the need to preserve local links. Some children have their primary attachments in one place but find continuity and other vital relationships somewhere else. There may be a major difference between a young person's wishes and her/his parents' wishes. The important principle of respecting a child's confidences may run counter to the responsibility to investigate the possibilities of abuse.

Some of the most usual dilemmas arise because there is a clash between short-term and long-term needs or objectives. For instance, the need for a thorough assessment (which inevitably takes time), may well conflict with the need to get a child settled quickly or to keep the separation of child and family to a minimum. Short and long-term perspectives will also be in conflict when the difficult decision must be made between the risk of moving a young child from a temporary placement in which attachments have formed and the risk of leaving him/her in what may be a far from ideal placement in the long term because the carers' age, different ethnic background or limited ability to handle problem behaviour.

There can be acute dilemmas, too, when the needs of individuals are in conflict. What should be done if differing placement needs of siblings clash with their wish to remain together or if keeping a large family together is likely to lead to long delays in achieving a placement? Or whose needs are to take precedence when a parent urgently requires complete relief from child care for a while to avoid risk of family breakdown, yet an out-of-home placement is likely to cause the child distress and at least a temporary developmental set-back? There may be clearly expressed differences in the feelings of parents and children, e.g. over the level of contact or whether the child should live with a particular relative.

There are no rule of thumb priorities that can automatically deal with these dilemmas because each child's situation is unique. However, common sense indicates that long-term benefits should take precedence over immediate needs unless the means of achieving them will cause lasting damage. There are some rather simple and obvious techniques which are also useful. For example, decisions should be made by a small group consisting mainly of people with direct involvement in the case but including at least one person who is knowledgeable but detached and objective. Listing advantages and disadvantages of a plan or alternative methods of achieving an aim can help focus discussion and lead to a properly considered decision. It has to be accepted that often there is no way forward that avoids all pain and disadvantage.

Actually applying individual principles is not simple either. It almost always involves practical issues, resources or actions of various sorts. The following are some of the practice implications which can be drawn from the principles quoted above and which have bearing on general placement decisions. Similar lists could be drawn up for other types of decision:

(1) If alternatives are to be seriously considered there must be a range of available placements (i.e. foster care should not be the resource.)

(2) Before individual needs can be met, they must be identified. This means that this particular child and her/his history must be known in some depth. (Careful history taking is not an optional extra.)

(3) Eliciting children's views and aiding informed choice involves direct, highly skilled and probably time consuming work with children, especially if they are very young or inarticulate or have a speech or hearing problem. (Communication skills and building relationships are basic social work tools.)

(4) The likely effect of a placement on family relationships can only be assessed if existing and past relationships are accurately known and understood. (History taking again.)

(5) Discovering and working with parents' views involves developing a trusting partnership in which differing views can be aired and plans negotiated. (Written agreements help clarification and consensus.)

Perhaps one could sum up the underlying message in this way. Just as decisions can only be as good as the evidence on which they are based, so the application of principles can only be as good as the practice skills and practical resources which are available and used. Principles are the colours on the social worker painter's palette. The range and quality of colour helps to produce a good painting, but it is the painter's skill which makes or mars the picture. Excessive caseloads or lack of the necessary resources can be as disabling to the social worker as lack of paint to the artist, but failure to understand and apply essential principles can spoil even the best resources so that they become damaging to those they were intended to benefit.

APPENDIX

SUMMARISED LIST OF PRINCIPLES

(*To avoid tedious repetition, the terms 'children' and 'young people' are used interchangeably and either or both should be assumed to cover the whole age range 0–18 years.)

1) *Children and young people and their parents should all be considered as individuals with particular needs and potentialities.*

2) *Although some basic needs are universal, there can be a variety of ways of meeting them.*

3) *Children are entitled to protection from neglect, abuse and exploitation.*

4) *A child's age, sex, health, personality, race, culture and life experiences are all relevant to any consideration of needs and vulnerability and have to be taken into account when planning or providing help.*

5) *There are unique advantages for children in experiencing normal family life in their own birth family and every effort should be made to preserve the child's home and family links.*

6) *Parents are individuals with needs of their own.*

7) *The development of a working partnership with parents is usually the most effective route to providing supplementary or substitute care for their children.*

8) *Admission to public care by virtue of a compulsory order is itself a risk to be balanced against others. So also is the accommodation of a child by a local authority.*

9) *If young people cannot remain at home, placement with relatives or friends should be explored before other forms of placement are considered.*

10) *If young people have to live apart from their family of origin, both they and their parents should be helped to consider alternatives and contribute to the making of an informed choice about the most appropriate form of care.*

11) *When out-of-home care is necessary, active steps should be taken to ensure speedy return home.*

12) *Parents should be expected and enabled to retain their responsibilities and to remain as closely involved as is consistent with their child's welfare, even if that child cannot live at home either temporarily or permanently.*

13) *Siblings should not be separated when in care or when being looked after under voluntary arrangements unless this is part of a well thought out plan based on each child's needs.*

14) *Family links should be actively maintained through visits and other forms of contact. Both parents are important even if one of them is no longer in the family home and fathers should not be overlooked or marginalised.*

15) *Wider families matter as well as parents – especially siblings and grandparents.*

16) *Continuity of relationships is important, and attachments should be respected, sustained and developed.*

17) *Change of home, caregiver, social worker or school almost always carries some risk to a child's development and welfare.*

18) *Time is a crucial element in child care and should be reckoned in days and months rather than years.*

19) *Every young person needs to develop a secure sense of personal identity and all those with parental or caring responsibilities have a duty to offer encouragement and support in this task.*

20) *All children need to develop self confidence and a sense of self worth, so alongside the development of identity, and equally important is self esteem.*

21) *Since discrimination of all kinds is an everyday reality in many children's lives, every effort must be made to ensure that agency services and practices do not reflect or reinforce it.*

22) *Corporate parenting is not 'good enough' on its own.*

23) *Young people should not be disadvantaged or stigmatised by action taken on their behalf,* e.g. as a result of admission to care or to special residential provision.

24) *Children's long-term welfare must be protected by prompt, positive and pro-active attention to the health and education of those in both short and long-term care.*

25) *Young people's wishes must be elicted and taken seriously.*

26) *As young people grow up, preparation for independence is a necessary and important part of the parental role which child care agencies carry for young people in long-term care.*

Principles in relation to Agency Responsibilities and 'Systems'

27) *In carrying out the duties and responsibilities laid up on them in legislation and regulations, local authorities should put into practice the principles of good work with children and families* which are set out in the previous section.

28) *The various departments of a local authority (e.g. health, housing, education and social services) should co-operate to provide an integrated service and range of resources* even when such co-operation is not specifically required by law.

29) *The twin issues of confidentiality and access to records need to be addressed by all local authorities and child care organisations.*

30) *Caregivers are entitled to have appropriate information about any child or young person placed in their charge and have a duty to keep this confidential.*

31) *Letters and documents which are sent to parents and young people should be written in language which is fully comprehensible to them.*

32) *Planning is a crucial responsibility for all agencies providing services to children and their families.*

33) *Agencies have special, parental responsibilities for the minority of children who are in long-term out-of-home placements.*

34) *When alternatives are being considered and/or decisions made, certain individuals or groups may need to be involved.*

35) Services to vulnerable children have to be largely provided through those who give them day to day care whether these are parents, relatives, residential social workers or foster carers. In each case, *a balance must be struck between offering carers support (thus building confidence) and holding them accountable for the child's well-being.*

36) *Caregivers – whether parents, foster carers or residential staff – need both practical resources and a feeling of being valued if they are to give of their best.*

37) *Appropriate training should be provided for carers.*

38) *There should be machinery for resolving differences of view* or minor disputes, e.g. through involvement of a team leader, fostering officer or other appropriate individual or through re-negotiating written agreements at the request of any of the signatories.

39) *Agencies have a responsibility to support placements which they have made.*

40) *Registers and records must be maintained and kept up to date.*

41) *Co-operation between organisations, departments and individuals is crucial* in the provision of protection for vulnerable children and also in ensuring proper use of available resources.

42) *Foster homes and residential establishments used for the placement of children should be reviewed at regular and suitable intervals* though this needs to be done sensitively so as to avoid undermining carers' confidence or making children feel insecure.